GHOST *of the* FOREST

GHOST of the FOREST

The Great Gray Owl

Text and Photographs by
Michael S. Quinton

DESIGNED BY DAVID JENNEY
ILLUSTRATIONS AND MAP BY MONTE VARAH

7.5M/5-88/0107

Contents

Preface

The gray owl lives in wilderness forests in northern Europe and Asia as well as in northern North America, where an estimated 50,000 owls make their homes. There are many different types of forests in the great grays' breeding range, and the owls' habits vary in order to take advantage of habitat. The quality of the habitat is critical; great grays must have natural wildlands and abundant prey and nest sites.

Great grays nest in the spruce lowland forests along the Yukon River in central Alaska, east to Canada's James Bay, and south to the United States border. Their breeding range extends south into Washington, Oregon, and California; in California, the great gray can be found only in Yosemite National Park and the surrounding national forests. A survey by Jon Winter revealed a total population in California of approximately fifty birds, which makes the great gray one of the state's rarest. The great grays also breed in the mountain forests along the Continental Divide bordering Idaho and Montana. The range extends south along the Idaho-Wyoming border at least to Pinedale, Wyoming.

The Yellowstone ecosystem, including Island Park and Grand Teton National Park, is full of great gray territories. Idaho's River of No Return Wilderness provides a place for the owls, especially where lodgepole pine forests are dotted with meadows. Greg and Pat Hayward located owls in the Chamberland Basin and Cold Meadows of that pristine ecosystem; they played tapes of the boreal owl and lured not only the boreal but also the great gray to disclose their mysterious haunts.

The nesting range takes a southerly dip out of Canada into northern Minnesota, adding just another bit of life to the forests. For over twenty years, Don Follen Sr. has been hot on the trail of Wisconsin's raptors, especially the great gray owl, and in August of 1978, Don reported, in *Passenger Pigeon* magazine, the sighting of a pair of adults and their four young, the first proof that great grays nest in Wisconsin, at least on occasion.

During some winters, especially those that cover Canada with deep snow and intense cold, many great gray owls migrate south to wide areas in the eastern United States. Conceivably, all of the states from Maine to North Carolina could suddenly experience rare avian visitors in their backyards. In the West, great grays are sighted very rarely as far south as northern Utah (there were several sightings in the winter of 1977–78).

There are many places where the great gray is

an occasional resident and goes on invisibly with its life, but the best places to see the owl in the West are Yosemite National Park, California; Yellowstone National Park, Wyoming; and Island Park, Idaho. The owls observed, photographed, and written about in this book live in the forests in and around Island Park and Yellowstone National Park.

Yosemite National Park. The only known great grays in California are found in the woodlands of this park and the surrounding national forest land. Look for the owls in Crane Flats, especially during mornings and evenings.

Yellowstone National Park. There are many great grays in the vast forests of Yellowstone. I have found them almost everywhere that I have spent any amount of time, including the area around Yellowstone Lake, DeLucy Creek, along the Yellowstone River, and the meadows around Norris. The chances of seeing the great gray are probably best during the spring and winter along the road from Mammoth Hot Springs to Tower, in the woods along Elk Creek, and around Phantom Lake. This road along the northern part of Yellowstone is open year-round. During the summer, look in the meadows around Canyon. Again, you will be most likely to sight them during mornings and evenings, when the owls are actively hunting.

Island Park. I cannot imagine a better place to see the great gray owl than along the many logging roads that criss-cross Island Park. For those with a real interest in adding the great gray to their

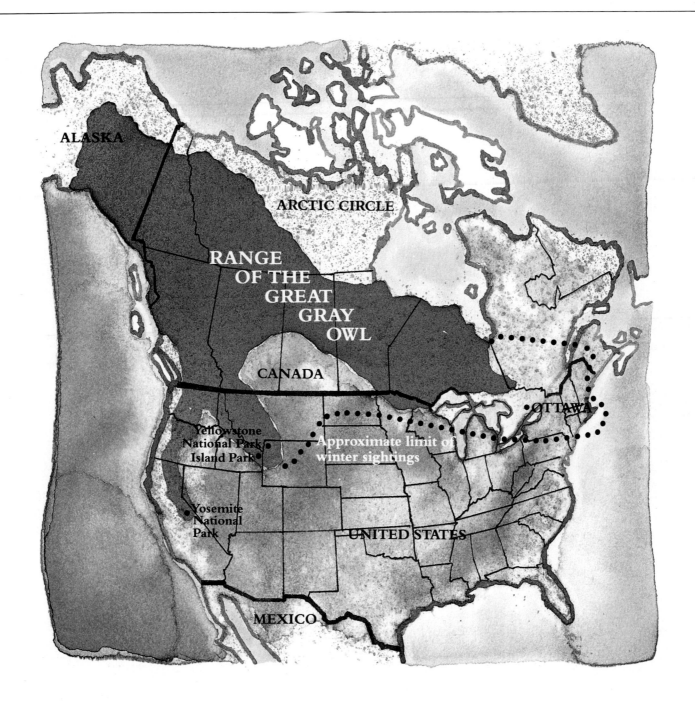

ALASKA

ARCTIC CIRCLE

RANGE
OF THE
GREAT
GRAY
OWL

CANADA

OTTAWA

Yellowstone
National Park
Island Park

Approximate limit of
winter sightings

Yosemite
National
Park

UNITED STATES

MEXICO

bird lists, stop in at the Island Park Ranger Station in Targhee National Forest and pick up a map; then, drive slowly along Stamp Meadow Road,* Chick Creek Road, Meadow Creek Road, and the Yale-Kilgore Road. Mornings and evenings are especially good. Drive the roads several times—the owls perch in the surrounding woods and thick brush and are hard to see. Your chances of sighting a great gray owl increase if you hike in the lodgepole forests or across the grassy meadows and around their wooded perimeters. Fall in Island Park is an especially good time to spot the owls. Stop often in the meadows that are adjacent to Stamp Meadow Road and listen. You can often hear the raspy screeching of the immature owls, begging food from the adults. If you are patient, you will be rewarded with the sight of an adult flying to its young with a fresh pocket gopher or vole.

In winter, the great grays are much harder to locate. During the worst winters, they can be seen in the cottonwoods and windbreaks around St. Anthony, Idaho; look for them in the evenings near the busy highway that passes near the town. They seem to be present for about six weeks, from January through mid-February. Careful observation is necessary, as it is easy to mistake the great horned owl for the great gray; the latter does not have the large ear tufts of the former, however. In the farmland around St. Anthony, great horned owls far outnumber the grays and can be found in the same areas.

OPPOSITE
A female great gray owl takes off from her perch toward the nest.

*Clearcuts planned for 1988 near Stamp Meadow pose new and unknown threats to owls in this area.

Introduction

The huge Douglas fir had been dead for decades. It had fallen over years before but still played an active role in the living forests. Presently, it served as a perch for a hunting great gray owl. Twisting skyward, a long branch gave the owl an elevated view of the ground below and the grazing elk and bison with their tattered coats of fur. It was spring in the forest.

This owl perched on the golden- and black-lichen-draped boughs of fir and spruce or on dead tree stumps and scanned the ground for the slightest movements or noises that would give away the location of prey. When the owl flew to another perch, red squirrels protested with nonstop chatter until the owl moved on or became motionless and forgotten. Once, the owl looked up to the sky and quickly drew his feathers in tightly against his body and stood up straight—the rigid owl turned into a broken, gray branch. A pair of red-tailed hawks sailed overhead; the owl angrily popped its bill. He had enemies, too.

When the hawks had drifted off, the owl continued his hunting. Gray owls can pick out the faintest sounds of digging, chewing, peeping, or rustling prey in the grass or under snow. There were eighteen inches of snow covering the ground that spring day, except where elk and bison had pawed and plowed it away to expose the grass. Here, rodents were common, and soon the owl detected their faintest movements. As the sounds grew louder, the owl's interest grew. He hopped off his perch and swooped downward. Just before impact, the owl thrust his feathered feet toward his prey but slammed into the snowy ground instead. He sat motionless with wings spread over the snow. He had missed. After a few seconds, the owl flew to a boulder, which, spattered with lichens, matched the color and texture of the great gray owl.

Soon the owl was off to a new perch. His hunting never stopped. Something under a small fir tree captured his interest, and he flew to a closer perch, one directly over the noise. Wings flicked and tail jerked as the owl made ready to pounce. Finally the urge was irresistible, and the owl attacked. He dove straight down into the tall, dead grass under the tree where the snow had melted. There was a slight commotion, and then the owl waddled out with his prey and hopped onto a log. The limp body of a small vole dangled from his bill. Reaching up with one foot, the owl gripped the rodent and began to feed. He ripped out a bite of fur and flesh and swallowed. After another bite, the rodent was swallowed whole, creating a slight bulge just under the owl's short neck. The owl glanced at me, then over his shoulder, then flew

off into the dark forest. A red squirrel chattered.

The setting for this owl's hunt was along Elk Creek in northern Yellowstone National Park, but it could have been almost anywhere in this huge wilderness forest. The Yellowstone ecosystem is stage to many such spectacles each day, although most go unseen, veiled by this forest and its mysteries. The owl is a part of the forest, a part of that mystery, a resident in tune with his surroundings.

Few creatures are more at home in the forest than the owls. Their cryptic coloration allows them to blend unnoticed with the trunks of large trees, and their nocturnal hunting habits almost ensure that sightings will be rare. Some owls, like the barn and long-eared owl, are exclusively nocturnal; others, like the short-eared and the great

gray owl, may be out at any hour. Because these owls evolved in northern latitudes, where there are long periods of daylight, great grays hunt as efficiently by day as by night.

The Yellowstone ecosystem is extensive and its habitat diversity is perhaps without equal. No corner of this wilderness is owlless; species range from the tiny pygmy owl with a fifteen-inch wingspan to the huge great gray owl, with four times that spread. Eight species of owls regularly inhabit the Yellowstone area; four other species have been found at one time or another. I have seen seven.

The mysteries of the great gray owl are slowly being discovered as scientists and researchers pursue the elusive birds in the wild. Not long ago the great gray was one of the least-known owls; today

Invisible to the human eye, a great gray owl sits tight against the trunk of a cottonwood. Feathers match the color and texture of the bark.

it is studied more than any other species.

The owls of Yellowstone and the surrounding wild areas nest in a variety of situations and settings, but they have one thing in common: they do not build their own nests. Many of the larger owls use nests built and abandoned by ravens, hawks, or great blue herons. Smaller owls use old woodpecker holes or natural tree cavities. They do not add any nest-building material of their own. Rather, they lay their white eggs on the wood chips in the bottom of the cavity. If sticks and grass are in the nest, they were probably brought in by another bird or by a red or flying squirrel. Short-eared owls nest on the ground, and burrowing owls nest underground.

The great gray owl nests that I have seen were located in the tops of old broken snags. The owls will, however, use any large nest available in their breeding range. In most nests there are a few long, downy feathers with the eggs, a result of the female's frequent preening.

All owls are predators, but the great gray is a rodent specialist. Only rarely does it stray from a diet of mice, voles, shrews, and other small rodents. I have never seen a great gray hunt anything larger than a pocket gopher. Larger animals are ignored, but there is little doubt that, should small rodents suddenly become scarce, the great gray could be a formidable predator.

Owls can see very well by day and by night, but it is their ears that make them such good mousers. In fact, scientists have proven that some owls can hunt in total darkness. They locate prey through triangulation of sound—dish-shaped facial disks funnel sounds into their ears, often from great distances. Triangulation is most effective when the owl is perched close to the ground, and helps them pinpoint the exact location of their prey.

Owls, like other birds, have crops instead of stomachs. Those parts of their meal that are indigestible—fur, feathers, bones—are formed into pellets, which are later cast about (regurgitated). Much of our knowledge about the feeding habits of owls has come from the examination of these pellets.

The great gray owl has few natural enemies other than humans, but red-tailed hawks and ravens are a threat, especially to nesting birds. Crows and magpies are notorious killers of owl eggs and young.

Several species of owls are mistaken for the great gray. The most common confusion is between great horned owls and great grays. The primary difference is the larger ear tufts of the great horned owl. The great gray's head is round and hornless.

I would have thought it impossible to mistake a snowy owl for the great gray until I saw an almost pure white great gray in northern Yellowstone near Elk Creek. The snowy and great gray are about the same size and may be found in the same areas, especially during winter when both migrate south. The great gray is a bit larger, but the snowy is a bit heavier. No hornless owl, other than the snowy, approaches the size of the great gray.

Perhaps the best identifying feature of the great gray owl is its large size: more than two feet tall with a five-foot wing span. The great grays have a very obvious white necktie, even in their white phase. But for such a large size, the great gray is a lightweight. Only the largest females (females are always larger than males) approach four pounds. Starving great grays have been found weighing less than a pound.

West of Yellowstone National Park stretches an extensive lodgepole forest called Island Park. It is prime owl country, a land of many hidden nooks and crannies, a last sanctuary for the trumpeter swan, bald eagle, marten, lynx, and other wilderness inhabitants. Clear rivers that never freeze are home to native cutthroat trout and rainbow-colored mountain suckers, which attract predators such as osprey, grizzly bears, and great blue herons. Island Park is also the site of predator-prey drama for *(Strix nebulosa)*, the great gray owl of the wilderness.

OVERLEAF
Gliding toward the nest, a female owl's slow flight is completely silent. Its five-foot wing span makes the great gray owl the largest in North America.

All afternoon, the female owl sat on the nest. Only her rotating head or the occasional breeze that gently lifted her tail feathers revealed that there was life on that dead snag. But now she was hungry and began to screech persistently. The begging stopped as she saw the male flying toward the nest clutching a rodent in his feathery foot. She hooted softly. The male landed a couple hundred feet from the nest in a tall dead lodgepole pine. He leaned over, took the rodent in his bill, and stared at his mate. She began screeching in earnest, imitating the begging calls of young chicks. The male clucked, spread his wings, and jumped off the limb; he flapped his wings a couple of times and glided effortlessly over the ground. Nearing the snag, he angled sharply up and dropped onto the edge of the nest next to the female. She took the limp rodent in her bill. The male turned, his bill red with the blood of his prey, and flew away.

With quick upward jerks of her head, the female swallowed the rodent whole.

RIGHT
A male perches over his mate with a pocket gopher, which was offered to his mate but refused. The male then flew away to cache the prey.
OPPOSITE
The male brings a pocket gopher to the nest, where his mate incubates four eggs. The female refused this prey, and the male seems at a loss for what to do next.

10

GHOST OF
THE FOREST

Half an hour later, she again started to screech when her mate landed nearby with prey. The sun hung low; only a few golden blades of light pierced the forest. With prey in bill, the male flew to the nest looking like a neon owl, flickering as he winged through the shadowy forest. The male stayed at the nest only long enough to present his mate with a gopher, which she immediately began biting with her powerful bill. She stood up in the nest, revealing a pair of newly hatched chicks and two unhatched eggs. One eggshell lay between the chicks, and another lay on the ground at the base of the nesting snag.

The chicks peeped faintly while the female owl ripped tiny pieces of flesh and fur from the pocket gopher and gently held their first food within reach of their gaping beaks. She also tore out a long piece for herself. After each chick had eaten a few bites, the female swallowed the rest of the gopher, then settled back down on the satisfied and silent chicks.

Perhaps no other part of the owls' lives are better known than their nesting habits, as it is only when nesting that owls can be continually located and observed. Nesting owls communicate with hoots, screeches, and an infinite variety of other sounds. They are often quick to defend their territories, but these owls are much less aggressive than previously thought and are even tolerant of other great grays near their nests.

Prenesting courtship is still veiled in mystery, however. Dr. Robert Nero, a Canadian owl expert, suggests that flight displays and pouncing on phantom prey are aspects of courting behavior. Perhaps the most important behavior in the formation of a mating bond is courtship feeding. I've often seen the male feed the female on the nesting territory. The female's presence at the nest seems to increase the male's desire to hunt, but instead of immediately eating his kill, the male holds it in his bill seemingly unsure of what to do with it. Upon seeing the prey dangling from the male's bill, the female starts to beg, imitating the sound of hungry chicks. He cautiously eyes his potential mate, for the female great gray is larger than the male and could easily harm him if she chose. With her attention riveted on the prey, he can safely approach. He flies to her perch and walks down the branch to within her reach, and she takes the rodent in her bill. Courtship feeding helps subdue the female's aggression and begins to free her from expending energy hunting. A trust is fostered, the beginning of a close bond. The courtship feeding leads to more intimate behavior and further strengthening of the pair bond.

Great grays don't mate for life in the true sense of the word—they seem to be tied more to the nest than to each other. I am reasonably sure, however, that the same pair did nest in the same snag for five consecutive years, based on the coloration and markings of the owls, the female's very aggressive nature, and the shyness of the

A nesting pair of owls engage in mutual preening, which helps foster the bond. The pair preens each other's facial feathers and may comb breast feathers with their talons.

13

A SEASON
FOR NESTING

male. At any rate, previous mates would seem to have the advantage of being able to form a quick bond, thus reducing the chances of a new mate being accepted. But in the case of death during the winter, there would be little or no hesitation to court a new mate.

The male and female were perched in separate pines about a hundred feet apart, inactive but aware. Juncos hopped and peeped about on the forest floor and in the trees, and chipmunks ran along the logs that stuck above the hard spring snowpack. The male lazily scratched his ear with rapid strokes of his taloned foot. Slowly he stretched one huge wing then the other, each with tips reaching a foot or more below the long tail feathers. The female flew and landed a dozen feet from the male on a large branch of a dead lodgepole pine. The male watched, turned around on his perch and flew to her side. He extended his short neck to its limit and began to preen the female's facial feathers. She joined in and they nibbled, nuzzled, and kissed. The male tipped his head, and the female preened the feathers on the top of his head. His eyes were closed. Then the male preened the female's feathers on the top and back of her head, zipping individual feathers back into shape. She started to comb her own feathers around her face with her long sharp talons. The male copied her and began to comb his own face feathers. The preening pair, leaning into each other, gave the impression that they had real affection for one another.

Mating is the final act that completes the long-lasting pair bond. Courtship feeding and mutual preening continue all through the nesting season and help keep the bond intact.

The regularity with which the male provides the female with prey early on in courtship could affect the number of eggs laid. When prey is abundant and the male is a good hunter, courtship feedings are often, and the female may lay up to five eggs. But when prey is scarce and hard to catch, feedings are few, and the female may lay only one or two eggs. In the event of an extreme prey shortage, she may not nest at all.

Nest selection in the lodgepole pine forests of Island Park is probably a simple matter, as suitable snags are very rare and are probably used over and over until the time when they finally topple over. Large stick nests are almost as rare. Ravens, goshawks, and great blue heron nests may sometimes be used, but I'm not aware of any in use in Island Park. Great horned owls also nest in Island Park, and because they nest earlier than the great grays, they have their choice of sites. The lack of suitable snags and large raptor nests are the main factors that limit the number of great gray owls, and for this reason, there are many places in Island Park that are void of breeding pairs.

In the mountain slopes, however, there are large stands of big Douglas fir. These forests are prime nesting areas for the great gray owls, as there is an abundance of old snags and stumps. Some of these meet the owls' requirements, and provide the females with a choice of nesting sites.

In the Douglas fir stands, many different snags are visited, but so far no one knows why one dished-out snag is chosen over another. Exposure to sun, wind, and rain, proximity to good hunting areas, a stream or pool for drinking and bathing, or places to rear the chicks after leaving the nest may all be important determining factors. The female will spend more than a month on the nest without a break, then another six weeks with the rapidly growing owlets, so she probably sits in each prospective snag before making the choice that could affect her reproductive success. Most big owls are territorial and will not share their nesting territory, so the female must also consider the proximity to nesting great horned owls and to other great grays. In the Pacific Northwest, biologists Evelyn Bull and Mark Henjum have seen active nests less than four hundred yards apart. At least in some places where nest sites and abundant prey exist together, the great grays exhibit very little territoriality. In Island Park, I have seen two nests that were about a mile apart. This is enough distance to avoid any competition between pairs.

Only a few birds nest earlier in the year than the great gray owl and great horned owls. I've seen female horned owls already on a nest of eggs in late February when temperatures are often below zero. Mother owls are tight sitters; they rarely leave their nests unless disturbed by humans.

Great grays usually start nesting toward the end of April or early May in Island Park, just as bare patches of ground are starting to appear under some of the larger pines. Elsewhere in North America, the nesting season of great grays ranges from March to June. Each egg must be incubated for approximately thirty days before it can hatch, and since the last egg of a clutch might be laid a week and a half after the first, the female needs to incubate for five and a half weeks before all are hatched. The male does not help with the incubation duties but he must hunt for himself and his mate. When the first egg hatches, his hunting chores increase dramatically. I never saw a female great gray on the nesting territory hunt until long after the nest had been abandoned.

Many owls that seem shy are quite tame around their nests. This is especially true of the great gray in wilderness areas because their contact with humans is rare and they have few natural enemies. Not even the sight and considerable noise of heavy equipment skidding logs out of a clearcut within one hundred feet of a nest would budge one female owl from her incubating duties.

Three to four eggs are laid a couple of days apart until the clutch is complete, and incubation by the female begins at once. The young will hatch a couple of days apart, the oldest being as much as a week and a half older than the youngest.

The eggs of the great gray owl are white, round, and slightly smaller than large Grade A chicken eggs. The female has a brood patch on her breast that provides necessary heat for the incubation of eggs; fluffy feathers several inches long are shed

also saw this and immediately began to beg. The male flew to the nest and gave the gopher to her. This time the male didn't fly away but stayed on the edge of the nest. After the female swallowed the food, the male leaned over and began to preen her head feathers. He nibbled around the edge of her facial disks and on top of her head. She then reciprocated, preening his head feathers, too. In two and a half seasons of watching nesting owls, this was the first time I'd seen such behavior take place while on the nest; it was repeated later in the summer.

Nearly a month after the egg is laid, hairline cracks appear and the tiny chick can be faintly heard peeping inside. A day or two later, the chick hatches, white and pink and completely helpless. Its eyes are shut and it still sports its tiny egg tooth, which has served to free it from the shell through scratching and weakening the surface.

Soon after hatching, the chicks preen their downy feathers with some help from the mother. Constant attention is needed to keep the feathers clean and in good shape. The chicks often preen each other and even spread oil over their feathers, which they get by dabbing their bills into the oil glands near the base of their tails. The oil helps keep their feathers from drying out and also waterproofs them.

Within four or five days, the owlets open their eyes for the first time. From the beginning they have very good eyesight. They watch with obvious interest the activities of birds and chipmunks.

The female is the most aggressive of the pair around the nest, but the male does his share of keeping predators from the immediate nesting vicinity. On one occasion I was laying in the shade of a pine right under the male owl as he rested, just a couple hundred feet from the nest. Every minute or so I'd look up at the owl just to make sure I wasn't missing some great photo opportunity. Suddenly the female owl started to snap her bill. The male immediately took off flying toward the nest. I jumped up just in time to see the male fly right into the side of the nesting snag about three feet below the female. Bark chips flew. I hurried to the nest where both owls were puffed up and staring into some thick dead pines a few yards from the nest. Finally I saw what was upsetting the owls so much. It was a marten. He was laid out along a lichen-draped branch half-asleep and didn't seem to know the owls even existed. The marten yawned and lay his head on the branch and rested. He catnapped about fifteen minutes and in between made his weasely growls. Jumping from tree to tree for about thirty yards, the marten then climbed down to the snow and bounced off through the forest. The marten was apparently lured to the nest by the smell of prey and had climbed the nesting snag. The alert female had spotted the weasel, given the alarm, and the male had attacked and chased it off.

The chicks grow rapidly and so does their demand for food. The male seldom lets them down and more often than not he supplies the family with more than they can handle. Very young chicks are fed by the female. She tears off small bits of prey and puts them directly into the owlets' ample mouths. As they grow so does the size of pieces the female offers them. If the female gives a chick too big a piece to be swallowed, it struggles in frustration trying to get the piece down. The impatient chicks peck at their mother's feathers or pieces of wood when they aren't being fed fast enough.

At first the owlets double their weight every few days, and within two weeks, dark feathers appear around their eyes. These rings are the beginnings of the facial discs that help them hear so well. They are starting to look like owls. The female is freed from her constant brooding duties and seems

OPPOSITE
The owl family portrait. The female sits over the newly hatched chicks while the male looks on. The male has just delivered prey to the female.

gets no special treatment, and when given a large gopher, it may take several minutes of intense effort to get it down. The rearend of the gopher may stick out of the owlet's mouth for several minutes.

The older, more vigorous chicks often get more than their fair share of the food. This was the case at one nest I was filming. The tiniest chick begged weakly and often but was ignored by the mother, who always gave the food to the nearest and most aggressive chicks. A couple of days later the tiny chick was gone. I suspected it had died, and the female had probably carried it away from the nest. During times when rodents are scarce, only the largest and aggressive chicks are able to survive, ensuring that at least one or two chicks will be healthy instead of all the young suffering from malnutrition.

TOP LEFT
The female sits on the nest brooding her new chicks and breaks up prey into tiny bits before feeding it to the owlets.
BOTTOM RIGHT
The male brings his prey to the nest.

to enjoy her new-found freedom. Now she can spend the cool hours of morning and evening perched in the shade where she can watch the nest. By then the owlets take up most of the room in the nest and they, too, probably enjoy the extra elbow room. As the sun rises overhead and everything heats up, the owlets start panting to dissipate heat. The female now returns to the nest to brood the owlets, shading them from the hot sun. Wind and rain always bring the female back to the nest and to her brooding duties.

When the female is off the nest, the male often brings the prey directly to the chicks or he may deliver it to the female who then takes it to the nest. I've watched one large owlet about three and a half weeks old swallow three big pocket gophers within a couple of hours. The smallest owlet in the nest

Mother owl delivers prey that the male has just caught to the nest. The male gave the prey to the female as she perched overlooking the nest.

23

All morning I had been following the male great gray owl as he flew from perch to perch through the lodgepole pine forest. He was the mate to a female on a nest I was watching and photographing. The male listened from each perch but moved on quickly if nothing caught his interest. Several times he was alerted by some faint sound of prey but each time the sounds died, the owl lost interest and flew off to a new perch. He landed on a low perch overlooking a tiny meadow dotted with small dirt mounds. He listened and watched intently from his listening post as I approached. It was evident by the way he stared down that something had caught his interest. Whatever it was must have quieted down because the owl's expression changed and he slowly closed his eyes. For the next half-hour he catnapped. I sat on a log within camera range where I could watch the owl open his big yellow eyes and gaze downward every few minutes. But, mostly he listened, then back to sleep he went. Suddenly he was wide awake

eyes, make them the superior gopher hunters that they are. The great gray owl has become so adept at gopher hunting that, in Island Park, they hunt little else.

The feathers around the owl's eyes function like dish antennae, funneling sound waves into the ears. The right ear opening is slightly larger and higher than the left, allowing each to receive sounds with subtle differences of volume and angle. This tiny difference is enough to allow the owl to pinpoint a sound's location by means of triangulation.

As long as the gopher is in one of its chambers, it is safe, though the owl can hear any activity. Shafts leading up to the surface betray the gopher, for the owl can detect when the pocket gopher is nearing an entrance hole by the increased volume of sound. The owl then has no time to waste, and with a quick and accurate pounce, thrusts a foot down the shaft and grabs or pins the luckless gopher. Quick jerks of his fist drive sharp talons into his prey. With this hunting technique, the owl makes his kill without ever laying eyes on the gopher. Almost always the kill is made before the gopher has had a chance to emerge from his underground home.

Rustling and chewing sounds in the grass and deadfall will trigger an attack. Voles, shrews, mice, and chipmunks are sometimes caught as they hide in the grass, but in Island Park, these species make up just a small percentage of the owls' total kill.

There are some moist meadows surrounded by thick stands of lodgepole pine where sedges grow

clip grass and small wildflowers, dip back into the hole, and stuff the vegetables into its pouch. Again it partially emerged to do more picking, then backed into its tunnel to stuff its pouch. This continued on until the gopher's cheek pouches literally bulged. Then it disappeared for the last time and pushed up some fine moist soil to plug the hole, not un-like a badger in miniature. The gopher is most vulnerable to attack while foraging.

The owls rarely see their prey until a kill is made. As a pocket gopher moves along in its underground tunnel, its progress is followed by the owl's extraordinary ears. True, they can see as well at night as they can during the day, but their ears, not their

THE FOREST
HUNTER

slow-flying great gray could surprise the alert grouse with any kind of regularity and the owls simply didn't try.

Day after day I followed the hunting male. He almost always led me past a clearcut adjacent to the nest into one of several stands of old-growth lodgepole pine. These stands with lots of big dead pines were rich in gophers and listening posts, a very desirable combination to the owl. He had several hunting routes that were used repeatedly. Each hunting trip varied slightly but ninety percent of his hunting was done on fifty percent of his territory. Many of the same perches were used over and over again. These perches always over-looked prime gopher country and were dotted with many gopher mounds. These favorite perches were close to the ground—from three to twenty feet high. Sometimes many pounces were made before finally connecting for a kill. He seemed to have his good days as well as bad, but success was always best when he could perch directly over his intended prey. From right overhead he could pinpoint the prey's exact location; the farther he had to perch from his prey the harder it became to make a kill.

Unlike many kinds of owls of the forest, the great gray that I observed and photographed hunted during the day; early morning and evening were especially to his liking. Some days the owl hunted all day; other days he was right on the mark and could catch enough prey to satisfy his mate, their chicks, and himself by noon and would then spend the afternoon perched in some cool timber. On

OPPOSITE
Overlooking a bar-ren landscape (at least to an owl's eyes), a male hunts from one of the few listening posts in a clearcut. Lots of prey but few listening posts make clearcuts poor hunting grounds.

34

GHOST OF
THE FOREST

An old, burnt tree is perfect for listening and hunting in the evening.

several occasions he didn't seem to hunt at all during the day.

Normally, when I filmed the owls from my blind during the evenings I would climb down as the light faded. But one day I set up a remote camera near the nest to get a different perspective and added an electronic flash for some night shots. I could trigger the camera and flash from my blind. Placing the remote camera had been very exciting, as the female owl had nearly scalped me while I was halfway up the tree close to the nest.

Just at dark the female owl started screeching as she sat on her nest, while behind me the male clucked. I heard the limb twang as the male flew toward the nest, no doubt with prey he had captured in the pitch dark. He landed on the edge of the nest, and I snapped a picture. For an instant the pair on the nest stood out bright against the black forest backdrop, but the flash was so fast I couldn't make out any details. Later, upon examining my slides, I could see everything I'd missed before. The male was delivering a pocket gopher whose cheeks bulged with fresh grass clippings.

The clearcuts in the owl's nesting territory were well stocked with gophers. The male spent many hours hunting in the clearcuts but his success was not good. Many pounces were usually needed to make just one kill. Listening posts in clearcuts were few and far between, if there were any at all. The owl often had to fly up to two hundred feet just to pounce. From such a distance he could not accurately pinpoint his prey's precise location, and a miss was almost certain.

Like other owls, great grays do hunt at night, although they do most of their hunting during the day. Here, the male is shown giving the female a gopher who has its fur-lined cheek pouches full of fresh grass clippings.

37

THE FOREST
HUNTER

In clearcut areas, the owl relied on his ability to fly; the trick was hovering. Upon hearing the sounds of prey in a clearcut, he would fly out and hover over the sounds long enough to pinpoint the source of the noise. His silent flight, made possible by the soft fringe of unconnected barbs on his wing and tail feathers, allowed him to hover and still hear the ever so faint sounds of the prey underground. A few seconds of hovering were followed by a divebomb straight into the ground. If he connected, a foot jerked as he drove his talons into the prey.

One morning I followed the hunter over clearcut and through the forest. He pounced several times without making a kill. He flew and I followed to a stand of lodgepole pine, killed several years earlier by invading pine bark beetles. He perched over a tiny opening of grass and fireweed in full bloom. I moved slowly into camera range with a medium telephoto lense, about twenty feet from the owl. A small commotion just below the owl had his complete attention. Suddenly dark brown dirt oozed out of the ground like a tiny volcano erupting—a pocket gopher was pushing soil out of his tunnel. Quickly the gopher disappeared back down his hole for another load. The gopher reappeared under a new flow of dirt and pushed it away from the hole like a miniature bulldozer in high gear. The owl just watched. I was tense, anticipating some great pouncing shots but they never came. The owl seemed captivated by the tiny rodent's dirt-moving operation. The gopher finally disappeared into his hole for good. Why hadn't the owl pounced? It was as if he wasn't used to attacking prey he could see. I think the owl was so surprised at actually seeing the critter that he forgot to pounce.

In my treks and wild owl chases, trying to keep the hunter in camera range, I often saw mice, voles, and shrews scurry along in the grass and dart over logs. Not once did I see the owl attack any of these rodents, even though I'm sure he saw many more than I did. He was gopher hunting.

In Wisconsin, Don G. Follen Sr., president of the Wisconsin Foundation for Wildlife Research, has been chasing hawks and owls for years. He has banded the only great grays in the history of Wisconsin. For three consecutive days in August, he watched a great gray hunting grasshoppers. The owl would perch on fence posts, tree branches, and road signs, spot a grasshopper, and divebomb to the ground. The owl hopped around a few times trying to get ahold of the hoppers. It would usually fly back to its perch to feed. Once the owl pounced on a grasshopper right in the road. A week later Don saw the owl again hunting grasshoppers but this trip it had also caught a vole. Don thought this owl had later been killed by a car.

One morning I was watching a pair of great grays perched in pines near their nest. I was waiting for the male to go hunting. When it started to rain, the female flew to the stump to brood her owlets. She had to stand in the middle of the nest and let the owlets huddle under her and keep out of the

OPPOSITE
A male dive-bombs to attack his prey. The pocket gopher was not in sight, but its location was pinpointed by the owl's extraordinary hearing.

38

GHOST OF
THE FOREST

rain the best they could, which left no room for her to sit down. The male started hunting. He bobbed his head, clearly hearing prey below, and flew down to a lower perch to hear better. He cocked his head back and forth, listening. A pair of tiny juncos, sparrow-sized forest birds, were upset about the big owl. He pounced and landed next to a large clump of grass and listened some more, concentrating completely on the sounds coming from the clump and ignoring the juncos as they protested and started attacking him. They plunged into his breast and wings in a kamikaze attack. Then the owl bent down, parting the grass with his large round head, and took a tiny object in his bill. He swallowed it. One desperate junco feigned a broken wing. The male looked up at me. His expression took on a look of fright and he flew off to continue his hunting.

I walked over to the grass clump and parted the grass. There completely hidden by the overhanging grass was a small grass nest. A single naked chick started to beg. The owl had eaten only one of the junco's chicks.

The year before, while in my blind watching the nest, the male came flying in with prey. He quickly gave the white, fuzzy prey to the female, who swallowed it whole. I could later tell from my photos that the prey was a small, downy nestling of some unknown species. It was inevitable that the hunting male would come across bird nests. He wasn't hunting nestlings but it was just plain bad luck on the part of the nestlings to have been making suspicious noises just as the owl perched overhead.

More often the male was attacked by birds who were protecting their nests from the big predator. One male robin repeatedly attacked the male as he was on a routine hunting trip. The robin crashed into the owl several times before persuading the owl to move on. The robin had managed to evict the owl without dropping a bill full of insects destined for its own chicks.

Most of the male's prey was for his mate and the owlets, but he, too, had to eat. Sometimes he would wait until casting his pellet, then eat the next gopher. He always took a few bites out of his prey before swallowing the rest because large gophers are just too big for him to swallow whole (although the larger female can usually manage gophers with one gulp). Once after he ate a large gopher, he flew down to the very last drift of snow left in the whole forest to quench his thirst. After a short rest and preening session, he continued on his never-ending chore of hunting for his family.

A male swallows his prey, a big pocket gopher. For several minutes, the gopher's tail stuck out of the male's bill.

THE FOREST
HUNTER

On 24 June 1983, I arrived at the nest in the early afternoon and started to climb the pole to my blind, when the female attacked. I had to jump down, grab a stick, and wave it to keep her out of reach. Before then, this particular female had not shown her aggressive side with but one exception: biologist Bruce Smith had climbed the nesting snag to check her recently hatched chicks, and both the female and the male had attacked. By measuring the eight tiny punctures in my back, my wife, Cindy, was able to calculate the owl's talon spread: eight inches by three; when pouncing on prey, the male could cover twenty-four square inches of ground.

When I did get into my blind, I could see why her behavior had so suddenly changed. There were only three big owlets in her nest. The fourth must be somewhere nearby on the ground. It must have made that first big jump of its life.

Just south of the nest, there was a small but thick patch of three- to ten-foot

A four-week-old chick in its first perch after jumping out of the nest. Although still unable to fly, this chick managed to jump and flap the couple of feet to the post.

this day without being attacked by the female. The chick was high out of reach, and the female must have thought it safe.

The owlet out of the nest seemed to get the first opportunity for food brought by the male. Only after he was satisfied and stopped begging were the nesting chicks fed. Seeing their sibling being fed while they sat hungry in the nest, the chicks were soon lured into making that long jump themselves, but it was eight days after the first owlet jumped before the nest was empty. The jump was not dangerous, but the landing could be fatal. Fortunately, none of the chicks seemed any worse for wear after the twenty-foot fall.

Each day the chicks would be perched in different trees progressively farther from the nest. The female still spent her time watching over the mobile owlets, while the male did all the hunting. When delivering prey, the male would land near the family of owls, and the female would fly to him, take the prey, and then deliver it to one of the begging chicks. One day, the owlets were perched just a few feet below an old woodpecker hole in a stump, which contained the nest of a pair of mountain bluebirds. The adult bluebirds were busy all day flying in a steady stream of insect prey to their own young family inside the hole. Their domestic chores were much too important to be stopped just because four huge owlets were perched close by watching their every move. The bluebirds ignored the owls.

A four-week-old chick climbs a slanting lodgepole pine to perch high off the dangerous forest floor. The chicks jump out of the nest before they can fly.

owls appeared in the forest as my eyes got used to the morning twilight. The owlets, though just as large as their parents, were still in need of their protection and skill in hunting gophers.

Owlets are dependent on their parents through late fall, at least, and sometimes until winter sets in. Evelyn Bull and Mark Henjum, Oregon biologists, have seen female great grays leave the family unit as early as three weeks after the chicks have fledged. The male is then left to care for the owlets. I've seen adults feeding full-grown owlets clear through October, when the coming of winter puts an end to owl watching for the year in the forest.

When fall is in the air, I have an unsatisfied urge to wander in the forests of Island Park. The elk are bugling, and the nights are cold. The bulls have polished their new racks and have to use them to keep a harem of their own. The red squirrels go into overdrive gathering cones. In the meadows and forest, the pocket gophers are active, too. They must store food for the upcoming winter months. Chipmunks pull down the long shafts and nibble the seed heads of grass stalks, leaving small piles of seed husks on rocks and logs. The tiny brown creeper, a nuthatch-type bird of the forest, patrols the trunks of lodgepole pines, going up, down, and upside down as it forages for tiny insects and spiders, then spirals back down around the trunk through branches. Love-crazed moose grunt along the rivers. I saw one bull following a cow and calf with twenty feet of someone's clothesline tangled around his shiny new antlers. Days grow shorter, and nature is issuing its warnings of another winter on the way. Soon the sun will rise to a world of white.

OPPOSITE
Waiting near the nest, a male with prey in his bill waits for the female to start begging before he flies to her with food.

In the Yellowstone ecosystem, and especially in Island Park, winter rules, and when it comes to which species will inhabit this wilderness, winter has the final word. Only if able to withstand bitter cold and deep snows can an animal make the Yellowstone region its home.

Chipmunks, marmots, and ground squirrels can't fly south each winter but they can leave the snow and cold. They snugly sleep the winter away in grass-lined, underground dens. Deep snows cover the ground and keep the intense cold out.

Mule deer, elk, and moose have for centuries used the same routes to migrate south for the winter to lower elevations where they can still find food. Many winter south of Island Park at Sand Creek Wildlife Refuge near St. Anthony, Idaho. Others stay in the hills near Ashton, Idaho, where snows pile up but usually not so much as to prevent small groups of bulls from finding enough food. Small

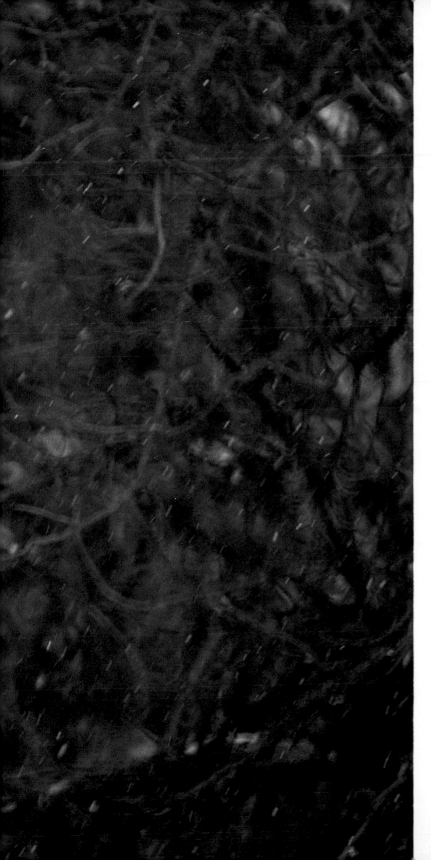

numbers of moose stay in Island Park to face the winter head on. These hardy individuals are tied to the spring-fed rivers and streams that are ice free even during stretches of fifty-below temperatures. The rivers are their source of food and their trails. As they move up and down the Henrys Fork of the Snake River, feeding on willows, fir, and underwater plants, the moose pass small herds of white-tailed deer.

Whitetails also stay along the warm rivers and streams, using them as travel routes. When the snow gets deep, they often lay under overhanging snow drifts along the banks of the Henrys Fork or in the shallow water. When disturbed, they invariably run off through the river.

Pronghorn that summer in sage meadows around Henry's Lake travel north over Reynolds Pass into Montana to winter in the Madison River drainage. Winter snows often come unannounced in full force and have often trapped the pronghorn. Many have starved unable to move through the deep snow.

By far, most of Island Park's birds are summer residents only and fly south for the winter. Only a few hardy birds like hairy woodpeckers, mountain chickadees, pine grosbeaks, and ravens stay all winter long. Clark's nutcrackers, gray jays, and the beautiful and noisy Steller's jays stay on during the winter, after caching food during the fall. Each fall the Clark's nutcrackers gather by the hundreds to collect limber pine nuts that grow high in the Centennial Mountains. They also poke their bills into the opening lodgepole pine cones to get at the

OPPOSITE
A male perches during a light snowfall near his nest.

55

THE FOREST
ABANDONED

A dark, perhaps juvenile, great gray perches in a tall, frosty cottonwood tree on its winter range in the farmlands of eastern Idaho.

GHOST OF
THE FOREST

tiny seeds in between the scales. Nothing is too small. They stash these seeds in the bark and cracks of trees where they can be retrieved as needed all winter.

Red and flying squirrels store food, too. In September, the red squirrels go into a frenzy gathering unopened lodgepole pine cones. Climbing a tree loaded with the cones, the red squirrels run out onto the boughs, bite off cone after cone, and let them drop to the ground. They then gather all the cones they can find on the ground and pile them under logs and deadfall. During the winter, the red squirrels tunnel down through the snow and somehow manage to locate these caches as needed.

Oddly enough, a few birds migrate from Canada to winter in Island Park, namely the rare trumpeter swans. Canadian trumpeters from Alberta join resident swans to winter along the shallow, ice-free Henrys Fork of the Snake River. This open water provides food for as many as five hundred of these endangered swans as well as many other kinds of waterfowl. Without these warm rivers, much of Island Park would be lifeless all winter long. Even warm-weather great blue herons stay all winter where they can fish in the spring-fed rivers, as do bald eagles and kingfishers. These rivers are Island Park's equivalent to an oasis in the desert.

For elk and great gray owls, Island Park is a summer range. When winter arrives, they make their way south where snows don't completely bury their food, although a great gray owl can plunge through a foot and a half of snow, including crust half an inch thick, to catch prey.

The heavy snows usually come sometime in November. My last sightings of great grays in Island Park for the year were of hunting birds. Perched in lodgepole pines along meadows, they listened intently to sounds under the deepening snow, and although they could hear prey, they could not penetrate the snow to make a kill. After that first heavy snow marking winter's arrival, I was unable to find the owls.

Some elk do not feel the urge to migrate at all, or the urge comes too late and they find the snows too deep for travel. Many of these elk do not survive the winter and become food for coyotes, ravens, and eagles, or a black bear's first meal of spring.

The great gray owls disappear. They do not truly migrate, but they do become nomads when food supplies become scarce. Some may stay in the foothills near the Henrys Fork of the Snake where it runs out of the mountains not far from Ashton, Idaho, but as winter progresses and the snows build up in the foothills, many are forced out of the forest onto surrounding farmland. During severe winters, the great grays appear suddenly along the river bottoms and in rows of big cottonwood trees near little towns in eastern Idaho like Chester, St. Anthony, Driggs, and Tetonia. I found them there during the hard winters of 1982 and 1983 but not during the mild winters of 1984–85 and 1986. That they do drift even farther south is without doubt and probably accounts for a few sightings as far south as Utah.

Great grays use fences as listening posts during the harshest winters. This male hunts mice and voles near a pasture.

THE FOREST
ABANDONED

My first winter sighting of great grays was on 2 January 1982, along the highway near Chester, Idaho. A week before, very heavy snows had buried the forest north of Ashton with over three feet of powder. For several weeks that winter, I found great gray owls in the farms around Chester. During the morning and evenings, they perched on highway signs and on fences in people's backyards, and during the day, they rested in big trees. These owls were at least twenty miles from the nearest forests in Targhee National Forest. Were they the same owls that nested in Island Park or could they be from breeding territories farther north, maybe even from Canada? I had no way of knowing for sure but figured they were from somewhere in Island Park.

On 10 January, I found two adult great grays perched in the thick woods along Fall River about two hundred feet apart. A few days later, I found a big, dark adult just a few hundred yards from the place I'd seen the two others. The owl hunted from fencepost perches and I filmed it as it operated. It would listen intently for hours from its several listening posts, but did not make a single pounce, for even here, on the edge of a cow pasture, there was still about two feet of snow on the ground.

A short distance away, another owl hunted from a frosty cottonwood. I walked under its perch and filmed it from every possible angle, but it totally ignored me. It didn't make any prey pounces, either. Later, it flew to a perch high in a cottonwood and didn't budge for the rest of the day. (This seems typical of great grays in winter. Once the owls found a place that was to their liking, they didn't waste energy moving around; they needed it to keep warm.)

A week later, I spotted another great gray perched on a pole along the railroad tracks just north of St. Anthony, Idaho. The snow was deep and covered by a two-inch crust that made even snowshoes useless. I plowed waist-deep through the snow as I attempted to photograph the hunting owl. It led me on a wild goose chase for about a mile to several perches, then flew up and into a small patch of cottonwoods as another great gray swooped down and nearly collided with it. The attacking owl flew away over the snow and barely cleared a barbed-wire fence. The owls' winter food consumption was greater than at any other time of the year, and I didn't know how the owls were getting enough food, as I hadn't seen any attempt to secure it, although many were hunting.

Later that evening, it snowed hard, and in the fading light, I saw more owls. Two were perched on road signs right on the edge of the highway, apparently hunting the barrowpits. They totally ignored the traffic. I never made a really accurate count of great grays in that immediate vicinity, but there must have been about a half-dozen.

After January, things warmed up and the great grays moved, I thought, back into the forest. For the next three months, I saw no more, until, suddenly, they showed up in their nesting territories in Island Park.

OPPOSITE
A male perches on a barbed wire fence and listens for the sounds of prey under the snow.
OVERLEAF
Great grays appeared one winter thirty miles south of the closest breeding territory. This adult stayed in a long row of trees in farmland near St. Anthony, Idaho.

THE FOREST
ABANDONED

The snowy great gray finds no shelter from the storm in this big willow tree.

The winter of 1983 was a lot like the previous one; a heavy snowstorm on 11 November was the last time I saw a great gray in the forests of Island Park. There was over a foot of fresh, wet snow on the ground and it was still snowing very hard. An adult owl was perched in a big, dead lodgepole pine listening for prey. By late December, more heavy snowstorms had forced the owls out of the forest and onto the farmland around St. Anthony and Ashton.

I saw an owl near Chester on 5 January, perching in some big cottonwoods near the highway. The tip of its bill was red with the blood of a recent meal. The snow was very deep, and I wondered how the owl had made a kill. Later that evening, this same owl hunted from fenceposts overlooking a field where a dozen cows and a couple of white horses were being pastured. The snow was trampled down flat where the livestock was being fed hay, and that's were the owl focused his attention. I saw it pounce once in that trampled area, but it apparently missed.

Several times in northern Yellowstone National Park during winter I'd seen great gray owls hunting over spots where the snow had been pawed, plowed, and trampled by elk and bison. Mice moving about in these trampled spots were vulnerable to the owls. Here in farm country, livestock was doing what big game did in Yellowstone.

The winter of 1983–84 was fairly severe, and all through February I found only a single great gray owl south of St. Anthony, about thirty miles from the nearest breeding territory in Targhee National Forest. Many times that February I found this owl in the same long row of big cottonwoods, Russian olives, and willows. There was a small marsh covered with cattails where prey was abundant, and I saw many tracks of voles meandering over the snow.

Once after walking the row of trees twice and checking all the owl's favorite perches, I gave up. As I climbed back into my car, I glanced at a thick willow tree a hundred feet away and there sat the owl. I had walked right past it no less than three times.

On another occasion, just as the sun was coming up over the Tetons, I saw the owl perched against the trunk of a big cottonwood tree. It was the best example of animal camouflauge I'd ever seen. The owl's feathers matched the color and texture of the cottonwood's bark to perfection. On the owl's shoulders were a few blond feathers and even these duplicated similar markings on the tree. Many great grays have these blond shoulder markings, which help to hide them as they perch.

One day it started to snow and blow a regular blizzard. The exposed owl soon found himself gripping to his perch for dear life. The wet snow stuck to his feathers, and soon the owl was pure white. His big yellow eyes gave life to an otherwise owl-shaped snowman. The owl shook his whole body and turned back to his gray self then flew across a field into some thick trees, landed on a branch, then walked down it to the trunk. He huddled against the trunk trying to keep out of the wind and snow but this proved to be only

During a strong wind and snow storm, a great gray actively hunts but is quickly covered by snow.

slightly better than the exposed perch he had just left. Again he flew off into the storm and landed on the snow-covered ground beside a large willow bush, which was bent over by the weight of the snow. The owl ducked and waddled under the snowy boughs and hopped onto a low branch. He was out of sight and out of the weather.

This owl was very tame, and I often got within ten feet of him as he perched lazily during the cold days. His plumage was all puffed out, making him appear even larger than he really was. He allowed me to climb the tree he perched in, where I filmed him from above. He did not get excited and didn't even give me a glance; I was simply not a threat in his eyes. But there were threats.

One morning I was filming the owl, who was busily preening himself with both eyes closed. Every once in a while he would open one eye to take a quick look around and once looked up just as a red-tailed hawk flew over and called. Instantly the owl shrunk his feathers in tight and straightened up. Moving his head, the owl watched the hawk until it was gone before settling back down to finish grooming. Later a crow flew past, and though the owl didn't fake a branch disguise, he popped his bill in anger.

Unless disturbed, and that was difficult to do, the owl stayed in the same perch, sleeping all day long. Every few minutes his eyes would open to the tiniest slits to check on the photographer or watch some little black-capped chickadees picking tiny bits of food from the bark of nearby branches. Sometimes the owl would hear the sounds of prey moving about under the snow or spot a vole darting across the snow but he never got very excited about hunting until late in the evening. About an hour before dark, the owl would wake up and start listening for prey, changing listening posts often. I saw very few pounces and figured the owl must have done a great deal of hunting at night. I did see places where the owl had plunged into the deep snow after some rodent.

When winter places greater demands on an owl's ability to stay warm, he must at times prey on more than small rodents. There are some records of wintering great grays preying on grouse, rabbits, and even larger prey. Canadians Daniel F. Brunton, H. Danner, and T. Dyke witnessed a great gray clutching a meadow vole in one foot when it noticed a white weasel streaking over the snow. The owl attacked and killed the weasel without losing grip of the vole.

During winter there are also cases of the great gray feeding on carrion. Owls feeding on carrion probably are having great difficulty hunting their usual prey.

While filming the owls on their wintering ground in farm country, I often jumped the big and speedy white-tailed jackrabbits. They were common but were not on the great gray's menu. Only the aggressive great horned owl would dare attack these big hares.

The great grays stuck to a vole diet during the winter months. As the owls hunted along the roads, they paid no attention to the big logging trucks that barrelled past, almost lifting them off their perches. Once as an owl sailed low across the road, it nearly flew broadside into a passing car. In an astonishing, evasive maneuver, the owl flew up and over the car. It was a near miss. Many owls aren't as lucky, especially in winter when collisions with cars kill many.

On 26 and 27 February, I looked for the owl long and hard. All its favorite perches were empty. Overhead, Canadian geese flew north and red-winged blackbirds sang from the stalks of cattails in the marsh. Spring was in the air. I knew spring was calling the owl back to the forest.

THE FOREST
ABANDONED

All the great gray owl nests that I observed and photographed were in the broken tops of huge, old, lodgepole pine trees. Sometime during their long history, the trees had snapped between twelve and twenty feet from the ground, leaving stumps with dished-out tops. (These trees break this way for a number of reasons, the most common being that they are weakened by nest cavities begun by woodpeckers; then, through rot, these holes are enlarged sufficiently to accommodate the small saw-whet or screech owl or perhaps a flying squirrel or a marten and her young.) Many kinds of wildlife depend on the availability of dead snags for nesting, denning, or burrowing. The bowl-shaped top of a snag is particularly perfect for a great gray's nest: the eggs won't roll out, and the nest is out of the reach of most predators.

All of these pine stumps had one more thing in common: when, as fledgling trees, they sprouted and began growing, they were located in meadows, either

as well as in other great gray owl breeding areas, the lack of nests seems to be a major limiting factor for great gray populations.

The lack of prey would also limit great grays, but this doesn't seem to be a problem in Island Park. There are pocket gophers almost everywhere, from the highest peaks to the lowest drainages.

But what about a forest out of tune? Like Island Park, many forests are being clearcut much faster than they are able to regrow. Some of these old-growth forests must be saved for owls and other wildlife. To counter the negative effects of varied forest use, forest service biologist Dick Welch is planning several new projects, pending congressional funding. First would be the building of new nesting snags, both in stumps and on platforms, to ensure future nesting spots for the owls. Second would be the placing of perching posts in clearcuts adjacent to known owl habitat; owls hunting in clearcuts have problems, because there are not enough listening posts. New posts would potentially increase the owls' hunting success.

The forest service is protecting some old-growth forests in Island Park and this should ensure a continuing and healthy population of great gray owls. Many other places around the country are also stepping up their efforts to help the owls. There are a lot of people building nesting platforms, not only for owls but also for eagles and ospreys. The costs of these projects, and others like them, will be repaid many times by providing people with the opportunity to see rare and elusive birds.

A five-week-old chick stands on an aspen stump and exercises its rapidly growing wings.

The future of the great gray owl is secure in protected places like Yellowstone National Park, but outside park boundaries, the owl's future is far less certain. It is hoped that greater awareness will mean greater concern for the bird's continued existence.

The great gray owl is a bird of the wilderness. Where wilderness is disappearing, so are the great gray owls. This is happening in California, where the only place in the entire state with a great gray owl population is in the relatively unchanged forests of and around Yosemite. But even that population is on the brink because it does not breed every year; only when there is an abundance of prey will the owls reproduce.

In Island Park, there are many times as many known bald eagle nests as known great gray nests. The bald eagle population is protected under law because the eagles are on the endangered species list; the owls are not. The nesting territory of one great gray owl pair is roughly one-half mile by one-half mile, an area of about one-quarter square mile or one hundred and sixty acres. This one hundred and sixty acres is being managed for multiple use, which means commercial logging, firewood cutting, cattle grazing, and pocket gopher poisoning (pocket gophers are being poisoned to protect replanted clearcuts) are all conducted in the owls' territory, including their hunting and chick-rearing areas. No one knows for sure what the combined effect of this multiuse program has on the owls, but it certainly isn't helping their numbers.

Should these forest uses cause the owls to expand into other areas, they might be forced to cross a very busy highway to more hunting grounds. If this happens the owls' direct, low flight would put them at the mercy of cars and trucks. This new danger would certainly cause an increase in the death rate of males who do all the hunting.

Cars and trucks on this busy road pose a direct threat to hunting owls and are a major cause of owl mortality.

Wildlife photography is in my blood and has been since I was a kid looking at pictures of birds and mammals in old issues of *National Geographic*. I remember when I saw a picture of wildlife photographer Fredric Kent Truslow filming birds in the Everglades, I knew that was something for me. Before that, I was deeply interested in wildlife; today, I strive to have all the wildlife experiences I can. This was the driving force behind filming the life of the great gray owl. In order to get a variety of quality photos, I had to work with owls longer than I had anticipated and it did become kind of a job at times (something I never much liked). I had to be at the nests early and continuously for three seasons and through all kinds of weather. Today, wildlife photography is very competitive and good pictures will just not do if you want to make a living at it: there is room only for wildlife fanatics.

My owl project began when I dropped by to see my friend and local forest

75

The author watches a pair of great grays on their nesting territory in the lodgepole pine forest of Island Park, Idaho.

GHOST OF
THE FOREST

service biologist Bruce Smith. Until then, I'd seen great grays a few times and filmed them still fewer times in Island Park and in nearby Yellowstone National Park. During a routine walk through a timber sale (forest area in which timber is sold to commercial logging companies for clearcutting), Bruce was surprised and delighted to spot a great gray owl sitting calmly atop a twelve-foot-high stump. Bruce knew well that I would not be able to resist this chance to see an active nest and I could hardly wait until the next day to see the nest myself.

Until I saw the beautiful setting of the nest, and the wild beauty of the owls, I couldn't have dreamed of a better opportunity and challenge for a struggling wildlife photographer. The sight of the female brooding the owlet on the jagged snag was about the most photogenic wildlife scene I'd ever seen through my viewfinder. I planned on erecting a photo blind right away, and Bruce agreed, as long as the owls didn't object.

The single chick was around ten days old when Bruce discovered the nest. With only a single chick, the male was not being overwhelmed with demands for food, and the nest was mostly inactive. The female brooded the chick for about half a day at first, during the coldest and hottest hours. A couple of times a day, the male flew to the nest with prey, usually pocket gophers. The owlet wasn't very large at two weeks but he had to swallow the rodents whole as the parents didn't tear the prey into bite-sized pieces.

A typical view from the blind.

I spent the entire day of 30 June 1981 in the blind with my camera focused on the chick, who was almost a month old. The owlet spent most of its time flapping its quickly growing wings and looking down from the edge of the nest to the ground. The chick jumped to the edge of the snag and back into its bowl over and over. It bobbed its head focusing on the ground, looking for the courage to jump. During the hottest part of the afternoon, the mother flew down from her perch to shade her owlet from the sun. Later that afternoon when the nest was again in the shadows, she flew back to a perch overlooking the nest and started to call in a raspy, little screech. The screeching went on nonstop, exciting the chick, who jumped around on the nest and flapped its wings vigorously. The chick teetered and waved with wings outstretched, balanced on the very edge of the nest, and gazed down to the ground. It appeared the chick was trying to muster the courage to make its first jump. It seemed strange to me that an animal soon to be master over the air was afraid of heights.

When I left that evening, I wondered if this was the owlet's last day in the nest. It was. The next morning, the nest was strangely just a stump; it had been abandoned sometime during the night. I found the chick perched ten feet above the ground on a young, bent-over lodgepole pine a hundred yards from the nest snag.

Since building the blind, I had filmed the nest only a week and a half. I was very happy with the photos I'd been able to get, and knew this was the kind of wildlife experience I was after. I realized I had to film and witness as much of the owls' lives as I could; the photo challenge of my life was still ahead of me.

The next spring, on 12 May 1982, my wife, Cindy, and I skied to the owl nest. We found no owls around and the nest was empty so we skied to another snag about a mile away, farther down the logging road. The previous fall, Bruce Smith had seen adult owls there and found evidence of nesting. The snag was in a rather open area with lots of lodgepole pines and a few big aspens. As we skied up to the snag, I saw the big, round head of a great gray owl peering over the edge of a nest twelve feet above the ground. While we stood watching the big female on the nest, the male came flying in and landed in an aspen a hundred yards from the nest. He was much lighter than his mate; she was gray brown and he was gray and white.

When the female flew out of the nest, I climbed the snag to see it. There were four white eggs laying on decaying wood chips in the top of the bowled snag. They were round and coarse. The base of the stump was rotting out, and the entire snag swayed slightly as I climbed and examined the nest. After I had climbed back down, the female quickly returned to the nest and settled on her eggs. I looked for a place to erect a photo blind about twenty feet away. In order to get a blind up high enough and sturdy enough for a good view of the nest, I had to plant a long, dead lodgepole about eight inches

A female owl sits faithfully on her nest. For a month, she incubates without help from her mate, then for another six weeks, she broods the chicks in the nest.

in diameter into the ground. I tied this pole into two standing lodgepole pines with camouflaged two-by-fours and then nailed a half-sheet of plywood onto the floor of the frame. My blind went up on top of the plywood. The female owl stayed put on her nest while Cindy and I planted the pole but flew off the nest when the hammering started. She returned immediately when we had the frame hammered and wired into place.

As we left, Cindy and I swung past the snag I'd filmed last year. We found one adult perched in some thick young pines and another atop a tall, dead lodgepole within a hundred yards of the old nest. The adults were in their nesting territory, and I was sure they would be nesting soon. When I got a look at the nesting snag, I wasn't ready for the surprise. There on top of the nest was a third adult owl in incubating position. Owls are supposed to be very territorial around their nests and aggressive toward any other owls of their own species. I wondered if this third bird could be last year's chick or an unrelated owl with whom the nesting pair was unconcerned. I had never before seen more than just the mated pair of adults at a nest. I still have these questions because I was never able to find out a thing.

Later that afternoon, on 26 May 1982, there was a violent wind storm. It knocked many thousands of trees over, blocked roads, shut down electrical power, and even smashed my canoe. I drove my car out to a big parking lot half a mile from my home where it would be safe. I worried all night about the owls. By daylight the next morning I was nearing the first nest, where there had been three adults the day before. It had also snowed five inches during the night, and I crossed mule deer, elk, and red squirrel tracks on my way to the nest.

There was nothing to be seen of the owls. When I saw their nesting snag I knew their fate. A tree had fallen into the snag, leaving it knocked out of kilter and nearly knocked down. The adult owls had abandoned their three eggs; two were covered with snow in the nest and the third lay on the ground under the leaning snag.

I hurried to the other nest wondering if the owls there had met a similar fate. Was my owl photography finished for another year? You can imagine my relief when I saw the other nesting snag and the huge female sitting on the nest staring at me. Snow covered the nest. Luckily owls are tight egg sitters, and although several big trees had barely missed smashing this nest along with my blind, somehow the female had stayed with her precious eggs. Her mate was nowhere to be seen. I wondered if the other owls would try and renest.

I climbed into my blind to film the female as she sat calmly on her snowy nest. The male never showed up, and for another night I thought the worst. Could he have been injured or killed in the storm? I filmed the owls from my blind every day. The male had survived and showed up with prey each day.

The weather grew hot and out came the mosquitoes in hordes. My blind didn't really fool the owls but it did keep the insects down to only a few dozen in the blind instead of the thousands that swarmed outside and around the nesting female. The blind did put the owls at ease though. They could go on with their responsibilities to the next generation without having to be constantly worried about my presence. The female was very docile, but that changed overnight with the cracking of her first egg. From my blind I could tell that something was happening. The female stood up over the eggs and peered down, cocking her head and listening.

Nearly a month had passed since our first visit to this nest, the approximate incubation period for great grays, and I knew the chicks would be hatching very soon. On prior visits to the nest, the female had always been quite tame and rarely flew away from the nest, so when I climbed the nest to check the eggs I expected nothing else. A photo of the newly hatched owlet was high on my list of photos needed to show their life history. When I started up the snag, the female flew off and landed a few yards away in a big, tall, dead lodgepole pine. Just as I reached the top of the snag and peered over its jagged edge, she hit. Her talons knocked my hat off and left me with a small gash in my scalp. I quickly checked the eggs. There were no chicks, but one egg had a hairline crack, and I could hear faint peeps coming from within it. I quickly climbed back down the snag gritting my teeth and covering my eyes, expecting to be hit again. She just perched a few yards away giving

me the evil eye and popping her bill in anger.

From that day on she never lost that look of revenge in her eyes. I was now her enemy. I knew that the chick would probably hatch sometime during the night but I also knew that I'd have to climb that snag the next day and face those talons again. (My desire for pictures often overrides what little common sense I have.)

The next day I returned to the nest. Cindy came along to film the female attacking me as I filmed the new chick. We were not disappointed. I wore a hard hat and leather gloves and when I reached the top of the snag I heard Cindy's camera whine. I held my camera up as a shield, and the female owl knocked it back into my face. There were two pink and white owlets and two eggs in the nest. Their eyes were shut, but when I snapped my camera, they perked up and begged for food for a few seconds before again collapsing down into the nest. The female attacked again and again, and I was barely able to expose a roll and still keep my head intact.

My brain is always in gear trying to get new and different ideas for pictures. For a unique angle of the nesting owls, I decided to install a remote camera into a tree a few feet from the nest. I could then get a picture of the nest and surrounding forest from an elevated position. It would be hard to beat for showing the owl in its nesting environment. I had wired a frame, which would support my camera, and was halfway back up with my camera when I suddenly felt a sharp blow and

The female attacks the author as he climbs the nesting snag. This female became quite aggressive as the first egg started to crack. Note the male perched against the trunk of a dead pine. The male never attacked.

GHOST OF
THE FOREST

stars began floating all around in the blue sky. The pain came a second later. My first thought had been that someone had snuck up on me and hit me with a big log. Years before I'd had the same sensation upon being smacked in the side of the head with a sharply hit softball during recess. I looked around as I held tightly to the small pine. There was the culprit giving me dirty looks. It was the female owl. Her blow came totally unexpected and nearly knocked me out of my perch. I shinnied back down the tree until she flew off to land near her mate. I quickly went back up the pole and attached my camera and remote cord. She didn't attack again but instead landed in the nest just a few feet away, while I double checked the settings on my camera. She settled onto the eggs, and I can only guess she had figured I wouldn't try anything stupid. She was right. She had my undivided attention from then on.

I climbed down and then up into my blind to get pictures of her with the remote camera. My head and shoulder started to itch and I felt something warm running down my ear. Not until then did I know I'd been cut by her sharp talons. There was a gash along my shoulder to the top of my head. After that I wore sun glasses and waved a stick when I went to and from the blind and stopped climbing into her nest. The ground around her nest for a hundred yards in all directions was taboo and that included the air space. Unfortunately my blind was within these protected boundaries. At first I was able to climb safely into my

The female gives a distress call when an enemy is near.

blind by waving a stick when she made a pass at me. She soon grew bored with that game and would then fly at me as I waved my stick, feigning one direction but coming the other. More than once I had to dive headfirst into the deadfall.

Blind work is my least favorite way to film wildlife. I'd rather stalk my quarry but that is often unsuccessful. There are many pictures that are just unattainable without the use of a photo blind, especially when working with shy and elusive animals. Blind work comes with the territory. Pictures come in spurts and there is a lot of time for reading or just watching the forest activity. I perched in my blind overlooking the owl nest for forty-five days.

Luckily the forest around the owl nest is alive with all kinds of wildlife. I watched porcupines slowly shuffle past the nest, stopping often to stand on their hind legs to test the wind for danger or maybe for the scent of another porcupine. One day I heard a snap and looked down from my blind to see a doe mule deer leading her fawn. The fawn must have been only a day old because it was very wobbly. The doe was nervous, she could smell me but didn't look up. My favorite and constant neighbor that helped pass many a boring hour was a small jumping spider. I usually ejected big spiders, wasps, and bumblebees (I'm allergic to bee stings) but this spider seemed friendly. Besides he hunted mosquitos.

When a mosquito landed near the jumping spider, the stalk was on. The black and yellow jumping spider does not make a web but hunts its prey. When the spider was within an inch of the mosquito, he would pounce. The mosquito invariably flew when the spider pounced and often escaped the jaws of death but it was never long until the spider spied another victim. Once after a careful stalk, the spider pounced and missed but was kept from dropping to the floor of the blind by a tiny silk dragline. The mosquito landed only about four inches away. The spider again stalked. When within his range, about an inch, the spider pounced again; the mosquito flew, but the spider caught his prey in midair. He dangled with his prey on his safety line, then carried his prize back up the line and took to his corner for a private meal.

My blind work ended when the last chick had jumped out of the nest. Each day the parents would be perched a little farther away, leading their chicks from the nest. Each day they were harder to locate, and when they could fly, I could not locate them at all. My owl photography had ended for another year. As I walked past the nesting snag for the last time, I decided to check it out. The area by now was very familiar to me but this time something was different. I passed by my blind and saw the snag. It lay smashed on the ground.

By the end of my second season of filming, I had accumulated a large file of pictures, but most

showed scenes and behavior at the nest. I had covered that part of their lives well, but that didn't tell the whole story. I knew I'd have to have photos of a male hunting and living his hidden life to have anything close to a complete life history. For that I'd need to know the whereabouts of a nest and the only two nests I was aware of were now rotting on the ground, home to nesting insects.

During the winter, I was able to locate a few great grays wintering south of Island Park and Targhee National Forest. They stayed several weeks near St. Anthony, Idaho. All winter I thought about where I might find a new nest. I had once known the whereabouts of a couple of nesting great grays, but after numerous trips into their haunts, I could not locate the nest. I thought about Dr. Robert Nero. This expert of the great grays in Canada had written about building nests in great gray habitat and having them take over these handmade nests the following spring. It was worth a try. March arrived, technically almost spring but still in winter's tight grip in the snowy Island Park country. Five feet of snow covered everything, but spring would come even if it seemed an eternity away.

On 6 March 1983, Cindy, Lupy, friends Mike and Kathy Jenkins, and I skied to the owl territories to search for a place to build a nest. We found a huge stump within fifty yards of the nest destroyed the year before by the wind storm. It was broken off about fifteen feet above the snow pack. All I had to do was climb the snag, cut off part of the top with a chain saw, and hollow out the top

for a dish in which the eggs could be laid. I climbed up and pulled the chain saw up with a rope. It snowed as I sawed and chiseled the nest into shape. Spring seemed a bit closer as we watched a pair of gray jays carrying beaks of dried grass into a small lodgepole pine. They were the earliest birds in this snow country already busy building a nest, but where were they getting the grass?

Six weeks later, I skied back to the nesting territory. Snow was starting to disappear around the trunks of the largest pines, revealing the casings and mounds of pocket gophers. In the distance I could see the snag I'd worked on six weeks before. There on the top was the round head of a female on the nest. As I skied closer she ducked down until only her eyes poked above. I heard a swoosh behind me and turned to see the male landing on a limb just a couple of yards above me. He hooted softly, turned, and flew away slowly, beckoning me to follow. I couldn't resist, and he led me away from their new nest.

I had to gain the trust of this male because I wanted to follow him as he hunted for the new generation of great gray owls. I refrained from climbing the nesting snag to look at the eggs and did not build a blind. I could build a blind after the chicks had hatched. By then I had hoped I would have many pictures of his hunting trips. I arrived at the nest every day at dawn. The female became used to seeing me arrive each morning and never seemed upset or tried to fly away. I skied around the nesting territory trying to locate the male. If that failed, I waited near the nest knowing he would soon show up with prey for his mate. Sometimes he hooted and gave away his location.

At first the male tried to lose me as I attempted to follow his every move. I would ease into camera range, which is quite close, and he would stare at me and get an expression of fear before flying away. Gradually he came to ignore me as he ignored the deer, moose, and juncos that shared his neck of the woods. From then on I was able to follow him and get within camera range without a glance. He was still able to lose me often as he flew about in the thick forest on hunting trips, not because he was trying to, but because I just couldn't keep track of him.

I went everywhere the male went. When hunting, he perched low and flew to new listening posts often. Once he pounced five times without catching anything but fists full of snow and grass. Once he had flown over a hundred feet and pounced under a small tree in a clearcut but missed again. It grew hot, and the male flew to a shady perch in thick dead pines, where he listened to sounds below his perch for a few minutes then slowly closed his eyes and fell asleep. We were about a quarter-mile from the nest. I had left my lunch in my pack stashed there under some deadfall and I debated whether to risk losing the owl while I made a dash for it. I decided to go for it, and found the owl still resting when I got back.

I had no more finished my lunch when the owl suddenly perked up and started listening to the sounds of some invisible activity below the surface of the ground. He flew a couple of yards to a lower, closer perch, which put him directly above the sound of prey. I slowly moved into camera position and sat on an old stump; a pounce was imminent. I waited with my camera, motor drive set on high, about five pictures per second. The male slowly spread his wings and dropped from his perch like a lead umbrella, straight to the ground. His wings spread out over the snow and dead grass, and he didn't move for nearly a minute, except to flex his left foot. Bending over, he bit his still-hidden prey and then pulled the limp gopher out of the tunnel with one foot. He tucked in his wings, glanced at me, and flew off toward the nest, clutching his prey. I walked over to where the kill had been made and found a tiny hole, the size of a silver dollar, hidden in the grass.

Among the fringe benefits of such a long-range photo project are the exciting and unexpected opportunities of filming other wildlife that always seem to present themselves. I was able to photograph weasels, porcupines, bluebirds, woodpeckers, mule deer, chipmunks, grouse, red squirrels, chorus frogs, spiders, elk, marten, and cranes, to name but a few, all while pursuing the great gray owl. But the best photo opportunities of all were those times when I was able to film some of the most intimate moments of the owls' lives, moments that are rarely observed let alone photographed, like the mated pair courting or the male stashing prey in a broken-off pole for later use. I

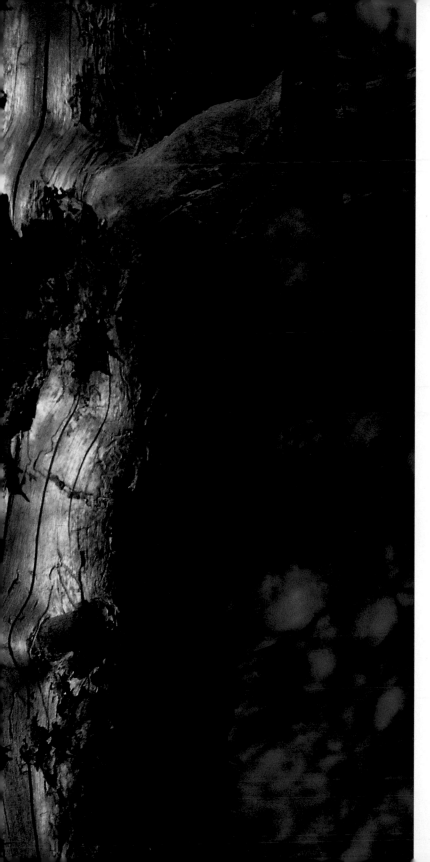

felt privileged at such times to share the moments.

Each new day that I followed the male was different and offered a chance of capturing yet another aspect of his private life. One of the last mornings I was able to ski to the nest was one such morning. Only on the old logging road was there enough snow to ski on, and the freezing nights had left the snow hard as ice. As I neared the owl nest, my skis suddenly shot out from under me and I went down hard on my pack. The male, who had been hidden, was startled and flew closer to the nest. He perched there only a couple of minutes before flying into the thick forest east of the nest. As always, I followed.

His previous hunting trips had always led me west and north from the nest so I wondered what he was up to. I lost him in the nearby forest so I slowly walked along a tiny creek that was actually a necklace of small, clear pools dammed by fallen trees. I heard gray jays calling close by and started their way when I saw the owl flying up the creek away from them. The male owl landed on a low perch close to the creek. I hurried around deadfall and thick young lodgepole pines to get into camera range. He stared down at the creek with interest, then jumped off his perch, lit in the tall, green, grassy creek bank, and waded in. He splashed in the pool with his wings a couple of times as I eased closer but flew off when I came within camera range. He flew upstream and then back down, and I was close behind. He would not let me get as close as I had been when he was hunting or resting.

Natural camouflage: this male owl blends with coloration of the lodgepole pine in which he is perched.

89

OWLS IN
MY VIEWFINDER

Once he landed on a log that had fallen across the creek and formed one of the pools. As I moved around some young aspens for an unobstructed view, I snapped a dry twig. He again spooked and flew off up the creek. I searched carefully up and down the creek and when I finally found him, he flew out of the creek soaking wet, sending a galaxy of water drops flying, backlit by the morning sun. He had bathed, and I had missed it.

He perched in the sun and shook his whole body: wings quivered, tail wagged, and head shook. He preened for five minutes before flying back toward the nest high over the trees. I found him later, still preening, in a perch seventy-five yards from the nest. I was disappointed at missing the bathing shots but I could understand his spooky nature. He was most vulnerable to predators at such a time because he was low in the creek and couldn't fly as well wet. From that moment on, putting him on film while bathing was number one on my list of picture priorities.

A few days later I was at the nest where I could watch the female on her nest and the male preening nearby. The male started to hoot. He called out a long series of single hoots, and I glanced back at the nest. The female was hooting too, her neck inflating between hoots. They were calling in unison. The male flew away, and I followed. He landed in the broken top of an old lodgepole pine. Reaching down into a crack he pulled out a pocket gopher, took two bites, and gulped the remainder down with a couple quick jerks of his head. He rested lazily for half an hour then flew east toward

the creek. He's going to bathe! I threw my tripod over my shoulder and ran after him. I walked up and down the short creek twice and searched the thick woods near the creek, too, but found no owl. A gray jay flew past me toward the creek and soon two more followed. It was that family of gray jays again. Soon I could hear the jays scolding something. I knew they had found the owl. Seconds later the owl flew right over my head toward the creek and out of sight. I followed as fast as I could and found him perched in a pine overhanging the creek. On cupped wings he dropped in slow motion into one of the shallow pools. He flicked his wings a couple of times, sending a slight shower into the air, and I snapped a couple of pictures. He looked at me and flew off upstream trailing water. He again perched over the pools but flew as I approached.

The male flew away from the creek and through the solid forest. I followed but figured I'd blown another chance to film him bathing. For a few hundred yards I walked through the forest and came upon another creek quite a bit like the first one. I was just in time. The owl flew out of the creek when he saw me. He flew farther upstream and out of sight. I followed. Wild owl chases were my specialty. After more hide and seek games we came to a large pool at the very head of the creek. The male perched over the big pool. I moved very slowly into camera range, careful not to step on any of the dead branches that had spooked him before. My five-hundred-millimeter lens would be too much gun here. I got a small telephoto ready.

OPPOSITE
. . .*then the rest
of his body.*
LEFT
*Coming out of the
water, he balances
like a tightrope
walker on the log.*

93

OWLS IN
MY VIEWFINDER

The male flew down and landed on a log that angled into the pool not ten feet away from where I stood. Without another glance my way, the owl walked down the log into the water until he was waist deep. Dipping his face into the water, he shook his head. Again he dipped and his whole body shook, sending up a shower. He shook his droopy wings and tail until he was completely wet. Then he walked back up the log with wings spread, looking like a tight rope walker balancing with a pole, then flew out, labored under the weight of wet feathers. It was a short bath, perhaps a couple of minutes long, but I did manage to click off fifty or sixty photos.

He perched in the sun and shook and preened. He preened all his feathers right down to those tiny feathers on his toes. Reaching back to the limit of his short neck, the owl dabbed his bill in the oil gland near his tail, then rubbed the oil into his feathers to waterproof his plumage. After an hour of hardcore preening, he started to hunt over some nearby bogs. He soon caught a fat gopher and flew off toward the nest with the gopher in his grip.

I walked back toward the nest filled with the satisfaction that comes from witnessing and photographing one more moment in the mysterious life of these wilderness owls.

Bibliography

Craighead, John and Frank Craighead, Jr. *Hawks, Owls, and Wildlife.* Canada: General Publishing Company, Ltd, 1969.

"Biology and Conservation of Northern Forest Owls." *Symposium Proceedings,* February 1987, Winnipeg, Manitoba, Canada: 87–120.

Bull, Evelyn, and Mark G. Henjum. "The Neighborly Great Gray Owl," *Natural History* 96, no. 9 (September 1987): 32–41.

Follen, Don. G., Sr. "Great Gray Owl Observed Preying on Grasshoppers," *Passenger Pigeon* 46: 141–43.

Nero, Robert W. *The Great Gray Owl: Phantom of the Northern Forest.* Washington, D.C.: Smithsonian Institution Press, 1980.

Reynolds, William D. and Daniel F. Brunton. "Winter Predation on an Ermine by a Great Gray Owl," *Blue Jay* 42, no. 3 (September 1984): 171–73.

Quinton, Michael S. "Life of a Forest Hunter," *National Geographic* 166, no. 1 (July 1984): 122–36.

Winter, Jon. Great Grey Owl Survey. State of California: 1984.

Other Natural History Titles...

AMERICA'S GREAT CATS: Cougar, Bobcat, Lynx
Text by Gary Turbak
Photographs by Alan Carey

IN THE PATH OF THE GRIZZLY
Text and Photographs by Alan Carey

MINIATURE FLOWERS
Text and Photographs by Robert I. Gilbreath

THE SAGUARO FOREST
Text by Peter Wild
Photographs by Hal Coss

THE TRUMPETER SWAN
Text and Photographs by Skylar Hansen

TWILIGHT HUNTERS: Wolves, Coyotes, Foxes
Text by Gary Turbak
Photographs by Alan Carey